ANiMALs AND THEIR BABiES

HORSES AND FOALS

by Annabelle Lynch

Contents

A⁺

Smart Apple Media

GROWING INSIDE

Baby horses grow inside their mothers. Baby horses are called **foals**.

A foal grows inside its mother for a long time. The mother's tummy gets bigger as the foal **grows!**

After nearly a year, the foal is ready to be **born**.

3

BEING BORN

A mother horse usually gives **birth** somewhere quiet and warm.

4

The mother stays close to the newborn foal to keep it warm and lick it **clean.**

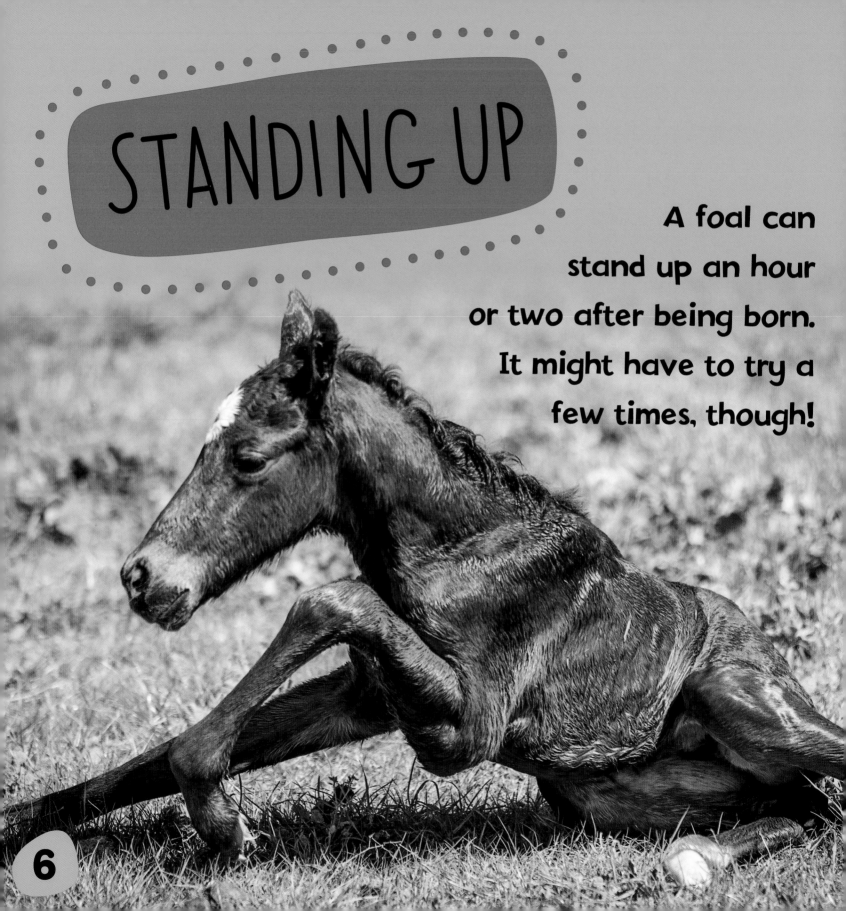

STANDING UP

A foal can stand up an hour or two after being born. It might have to try a few times, though!

Later that same day, the foal can walk and even run.

Clip! Clop!

7

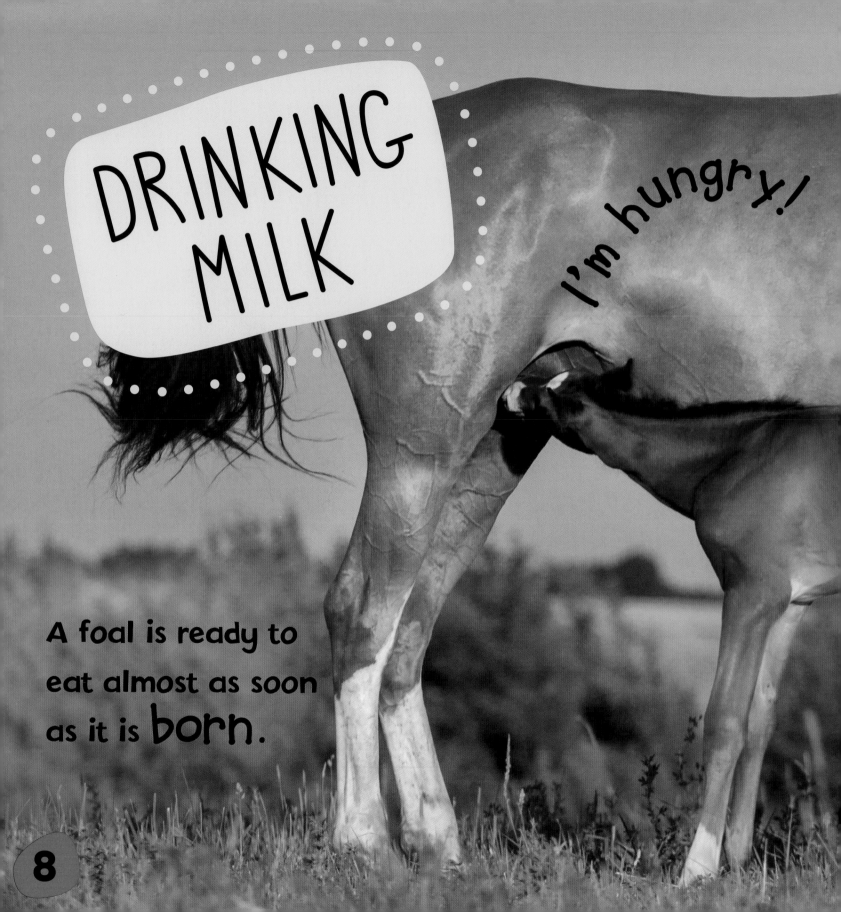

DRINKING MILK

I'm hungry!

A foal is ready to eat almost as soon as it is **born**.

8

It sucks milk from its mother's teats. Foals drink their mothers' milk until they are about six months old or even older.

GRAZING

When a foal is a few weeks old, it starts eating grass. This is called grazing. It begins drinking water too.

Grass is a horse's favorite food.

But it also likes
eating hay,
oats, and apples.

LEGS AND HOOVES

A newborn foal has very long legs. It is almost as **tall** as an adult horse!

12

A foal has **four** hooves. Its hooves are soft when it's born, but they get harder. Hooves need to be kept healthy so the foal can walk properly as it grows up.

13

BROWN, BLACK, OR SPOTTED

Foals are covered in soft, thick coats of hair.

The hair can be brown, black, gray, white, or **spotted**. Foals are usually, but not always, the same colors as their mothers.

Foals and horses have thick hair growing out of their necks.

This hair is called a mane.

15

PLAY AND REST

As foals grow up, they should run and play outside every day. Playing helps them have **strong** and **healthy** bodies.

After play,
foals need
to get lots of
rest too!

Z
Z
Z
z
z

17

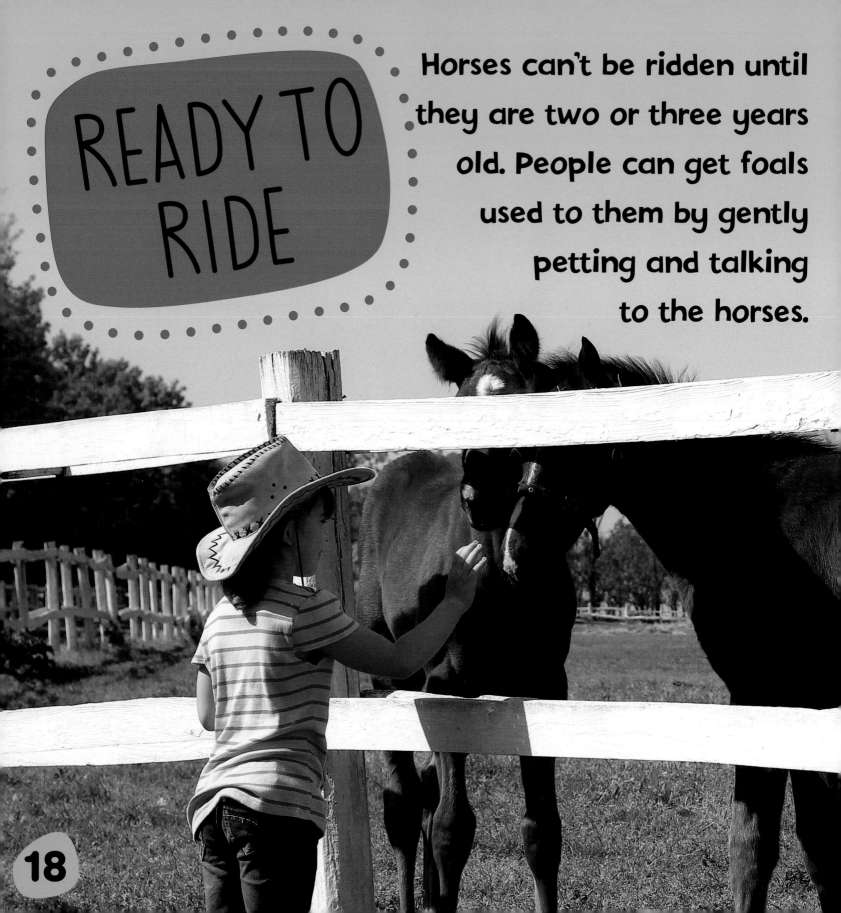

READY TO RIDE

Horses can't be ridden until they are two or three years old. People can get foals used to them by gently petting and talking to the horses.

When they are ready, people can try leading foals using **halters.**

A GROWN-UP HORSE

When a foal is a year old, it is called a **yearling**. Many yearlings are ready to leave their mothers and go to new homes. Others stay with their mothers all their lives.

When a horse
is around three
years old, it is ready to
have foals of its own.

21

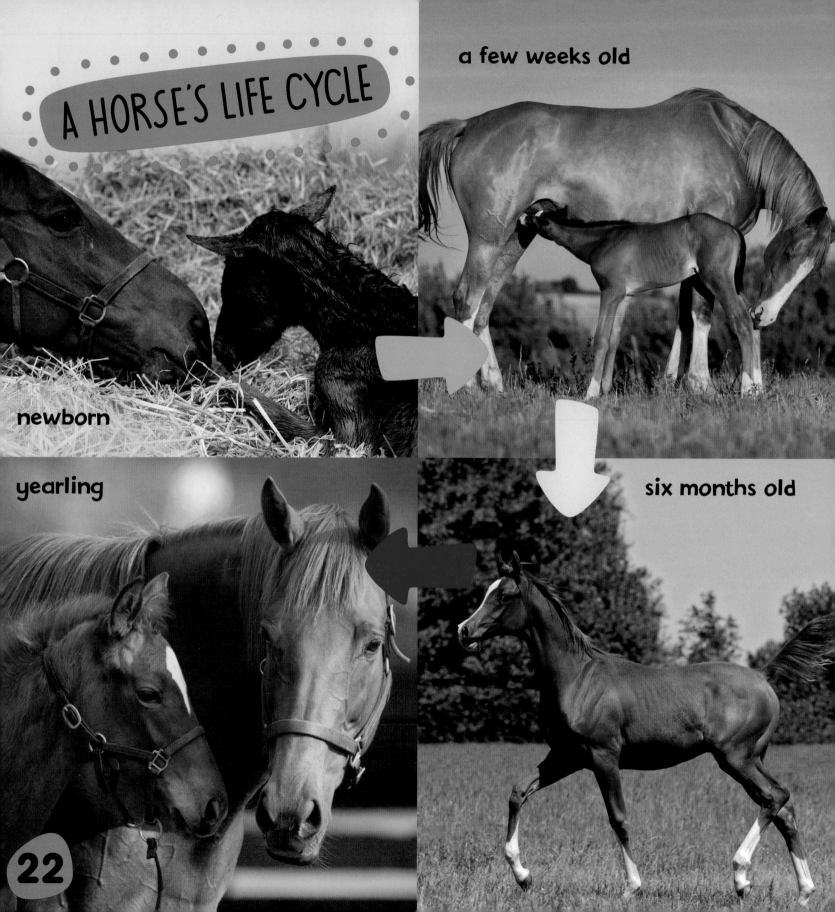

A HORSE'S LIFE CYCLE

a few weeks old

newborn

six months old

yearling

22

grazing

halter

hoof

mane

WORD
BANK

newborn

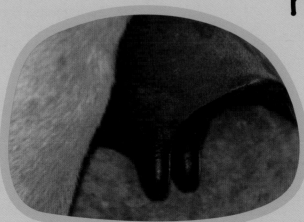

teats

23

INDEX

Published by Smart Apple Media, an imprint of Black Rabbit Books
P.O. Box 3263, Mankato, Minnesota 56002

U.S. publication copyright © 2017 Smart Apple Media. All rights reserved. International copyright reserved in all countries. No part of this book may be reproduced in any form without written permission from the publisher.

Published by arrangement with Watts Publishing, London.

Cataloging-in-Publication Data is on file with the Library of Congress.
ISBN: 978-1-62588-417-6
eISBN: 978-1-62588-421-3

Picture credits: blickwinkel/Lenz/Alamy: 23b. Agencia Fotograficzna Caro/Alamy: 4-5, 22tl, 23cr. Lars Christensen/Dreamstime: 10, 23tl. Manfred Grebler/Alamy: 22br. Svetlana Golubenko/Dreamstime: 8-9, 22tr. imagebroker/Alamy: 11. Kathryn Thorpe Klassen/Alamy: 17. Holly Kuchera/Shutterstock: 19, 23tc. mariait/Shutterstock: 16. Janian Mcmillan/Dreamstime: 6, 24. mkant/Shutterstock: 1bl, 7. Red Photography/Dreamstime: 1tr, 13, 23tr. Goce Risteski/Dreamstime: 18. Conny Sjostrom/Shutterstock: 2-3. smereka/Shutterstock: front cover. Kent Weakley/Shutterstock: 20-21, 22bl. Zoonar GmbH/Alamy: 12. Zuzule/Shutterstock: 14-15, 23cl.

Every attempt has been made to clear copyright. Should there be any inadvertent omission please apply to the publisher for rectification.

Printed in the United States by CG Book Printers North Mankato, Minnesota

PO 1776

3-2016